13

TO MY SONS

TO MY SONS

LESSONS FOR THE WILD ADVENTURE
CALLED LIFE

BEAR GRYLLS

David C Cook

transforming lives together

TO MY SONS
Published by David C Cook
4050 Lee Vance View
Colorado Springs, CO 80918 U.S.A.

David C Cook Distribution Canada
55 Woodslee Avenue, Paris, Ontario, Canada N3L 3E5

David C Cook U.K., Kingsway Communications
Eastbourne, East Sussex BN23 6NT, England

The graphic circle C logo is a registered trademark of David C Cook.

Unless otherwise noted, all Scripture quotations are taken from the Holy
Bible, New International Version®, NIV®. Copyright © 1973, 1978, 1984 by
Biblica, Inc.™ Used by permission of Zondervan. All rights reserved worldwide.
www.zondervan.com. Scripture quotations marked NCV are taken from the
New Century Version. Copyright © 1987, 1988, 1991 by Word Publishing,
a division of Thomas Nelson, Inc. Used by permission. All rights reserved.
Scripture quotations marked NKJV are taken from the New King James Version.
Copyright © 1982 by Thomas Nelson, Inc. Used by permission. All rights
reserved. Scripture quotations marked NLT are taken from the New Living
Translation of the Holy Bible. New Living Translation copyright © 1996, 2004
by Tyndale Charitable Trust. Used by permission of Tyndale House Publishers.

LCCN 2011937599
ISBN 978-1-4347-0358-3
eISBN 978-0-7814-0801-1

© 2012 Bear Grylls
Published by arrangement with Alpha International.
First UK edition published as *With Love, Papa* in 2009 by
Lion Hudson © Bear Grylls, ISBN 978-0-7459-5501-8

The Team: Alex Field, Nick Lee, Renada Arens, Karen Athen
Cover Design: Amy Konyndyk
Cover Photo: Discovery Communications, LLC
Illustrations: Charlie Mackesy

Printed in the United States of America
First North American Edition 2012

1 2 3 4 5 6 7 8 9 10

101711

PREFACE

To my sons, the great joy in my life.

This little book is a culmination of all that I have learned about the game of life. I have learned these simple truths through many mistakes and many falls. I have learned them from watching and being around those I love and admire, and I have learned them through the hard times that life sometimes throws at us.

I have also learned that what I value most is found close at home: just being with you three boys and your mama.

I hope these simple truths help you blossom in the game of life, and I hope they help you follow your hearts and many dreams. I hope they remind you to cherish those close to you and to live boldly and with a smile.

You are the most wonderful joy in both our lives, and I could never have imagined such good fortune to be able to hold you close to me so often (although it never seems enough!).

I adore you and am oh, so proud of you. You are the best.

With love,

Papa

Aim to live a wild, generous, full, exciting life—blessing those around you and seeing the good in all.

———

Follow your dreams—they are God given.

Have a few close friends who you see often—their friendship matters more than having many shallow acquaintances.

———

Be honest and vulnerable with those close to you. It creates strong bonds.

"I think I'm addicted to Chocolate"

"me too"

"and girls"

"me too"

Don't be held back,
either by fear or by lack
of confidence. Go for
it, despite these very
normal emotions that
we all feel occasionally.

Build people up.

Be faithful—any old slime can cheat!

Smile and laugh
more than is
considered normal!

Be loyal—it is the
mark of a man.

"...personally I like his dress sense"

Remember the verse,
"We are the sweet
smell of Christ among
those who are being
saved and among those
who are being lost."
(2 Corinthians 2:15 NCV)

Exercise at least every other day—make it a habit. Then you will shine even brighter.

Choose your job carefully—do work that excites you. It is where you will spend so much of your time.

"Another dull day at
the office"

Don't be afraid to be
weak occasionally.

Choose a job that
betters people's lives.

Snack on nuts and fruit—
they suppress appetite
and make you strong!

———

Remember the verse, "I
can do all things through
Christ who strengthens me"
(Philippians 4:13 NKJV).

Cheerfulness in adversity
is a key character trait
in the game of life.

Moments of doubt
are part of life. Accept
them and remember
that Jesus Himself said,
"My power is made
perfect in weakness"
(2 Corinthians 12:9).

Nobility is not a birthright—how we act in the big moments defines who we are.

Encourage, encourage;
help, help.

Remember this verse by heart:
"Even there your hand will
guide me, your right hand will
hold me fast" (Psalm 139:10).

―――

Understand that failure is
an essential stepping-stone
on the road to success.

"OK, so this puddle
is to be avoided next time"

Always keep the big picture in mind—you are greatly loved by Jesus and your job is to love Him and others in return. The rest is detail.

"That's a big picture"

Give more than you
take, especially with friends and
family. See the best in people—
as Christ does with you.

———

Compliment people—kind
words can change lives, and
people rarely forget.

"one for me,
two for you"

Manners really matter; in fact, they make the man.

Remember that how you
speak about others speaks
loudest about yourself.

———

If you want to see the real man,
give him power over people and
see what he does. Remember
this in how you treat people.

Be the most enthusiastic
person you know!

———

Love Jesus.

———

Find a fun, honest, down-to-earth
local church and support it.

Be gentle.

———

Consider others better
than yourself.

———

Be especially kind, thoughtful,
and generous to those who
are overlooked in life—this is
the measure of a real man.

Pray daily—what a person the
Lord is to have helping you!

———

Be courageous in key moments.

Eat lots of fruit and vegetables. They fight all the free radicals that try to slow you down.

Be kind to those whom
others neglect.

———

If supply is short, then look
for something to give away. It
is a law of the universe—to
receive you must first give.

Put 10 percent of your income aside and give that money to those in need—whether friends or charities. You have the power to save lives.

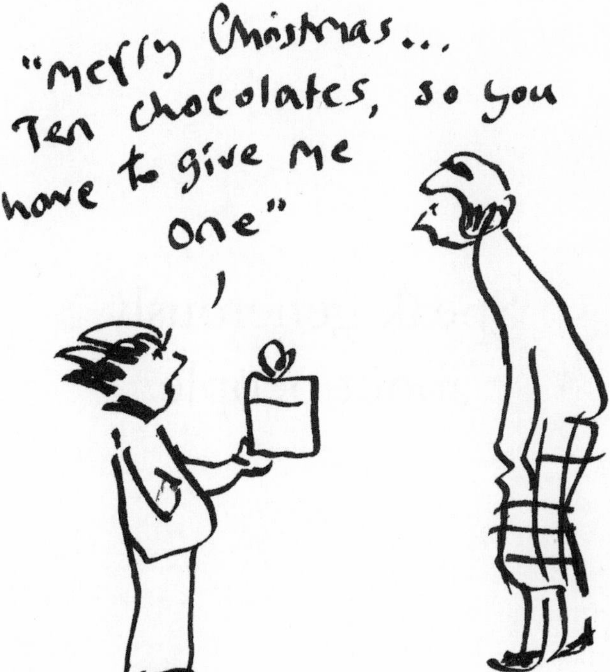
"Merry Christmas...
Ten chocolates, so you
have to give me
one"

Speak generously
about people.

"I know he shot the gamekeeper...
but what a shot!"

Sometimes it is worth losing a battle to win the war.

Jesus came to seek
and to save us—let
Him do His job!

Help friends in need.

———

Don't lend money; rather, give it.

"Thanks"

Say "why not?"
rather than "why?"

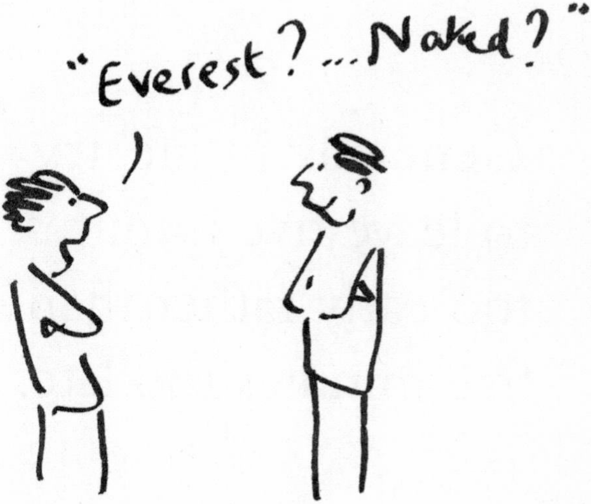
"Everest? ... Naked?"

Generally in life, try to leave five minutes too early rather than five minutes too late.

"The alarm didn't go off"

The people to be nicest
to in life are your wife
and your children—
give them the most
time, energy, and love,
and you will be happy.

Spend more time with your family and less at work—no one on their deathbed says they wish they had spent more time in the office!

Marry only for love.

This is a great one to remember: "And be sure of this: I am with you always, even to the end of the age" (Matthew 28:20 NLT).
I had this engraved on Mama's wedding ring when we married!

———

Lead by example.

"walk this way, please"

Preach Jesus every day—when necessary, use words! That is, love and listen to people.

No one cares how much
you know until they know
how much you care.

———

Don't lie.

You have two ears and one mouth—use them in proportion: Listen twice as much as you speak!

Don't one-up
people's stories.

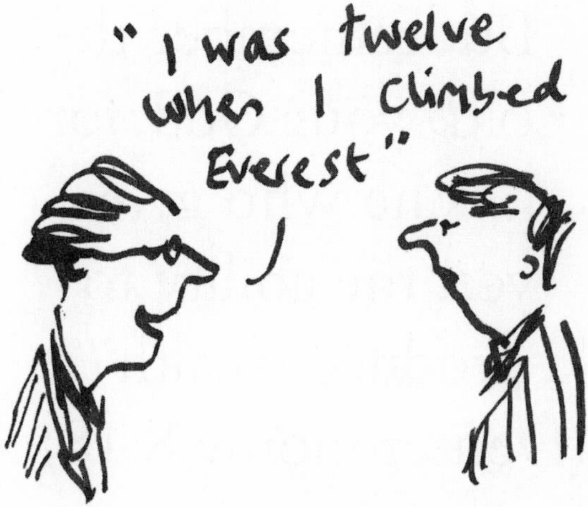
"I was twelve when I climbed Everest"

"But remember the
LORD your God, for
it is he who gives
you the ability to
produce wealth"
(Deuteronomy 8:18).

Thank God for your many blessings; then go out there and blossom. It is okay to succeed!

Always look people
in the eye.

Have a firm handshake.

When you call
someone, first ask if it
is a good time to talk.

Don't be afraid to be quiet
and let others shine.

———

Treat others as you would
like to be treated.

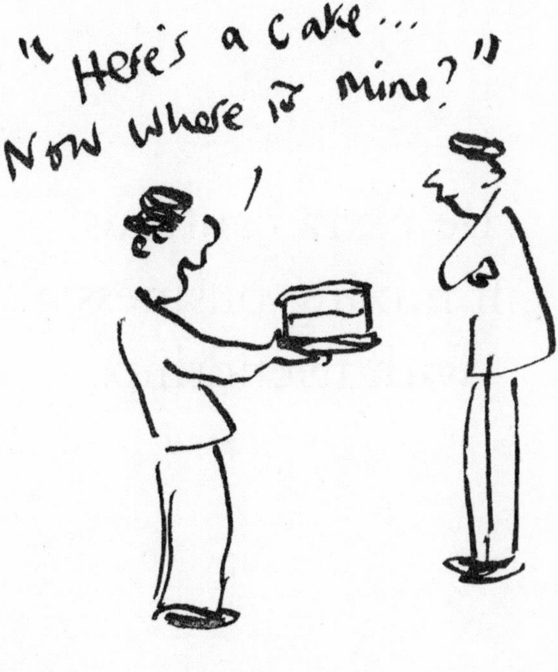
"Here's a cake... Now where is mine?"

Be extra cautious
if mixing business
with friendship.

Pride comes before a fall—so don't be too proud to let others win. There is room for everyone to do well!

Be ambitious—think big and take calculated risks.

Be open, honest, and
fair in all your dealings.

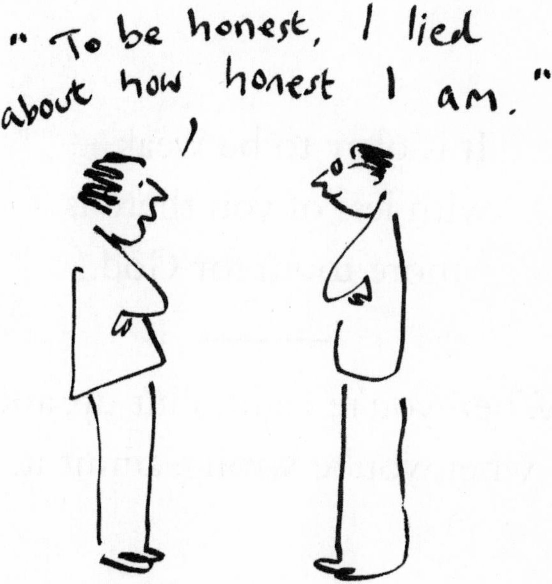
" To be honest, I lied about how honest I am."

It is okay to be weak—
with less of you there is
more room for God.

———

When you're right, shut up, and
when you're wrong, admit it.

101

Many great people over the centuries have depended on their faith—it is a sign of great strength to need Jesus in your life.

Be the first to apologize.

Enjoy the silence.

Make a little time to
be quiet by yourself
every day and just be.

Don't go to battle unless it is absolutely necessary—to turn the other cheek takes great strength and courage.

"Here's my other cheek."

Crying is healthy!

———

Always hold hands with
those you love whenever
you have the chance.

———

Gratitude, gratitude, gratitude.

Relax. You have no need for the common concerns of life. Remember Isaiah: "The LORD will guide you always" (58:11).

———

Don't worry about anything that is outside your sphere of influence—if you can't change it, don't waste time worrying about it!

Learn a few clean jokes
and a good card trick.

117

Laugh at yourself.

Learn to play an
instrument.

Swim in streams. Be
spontaneous—it's fun!

———

Watch a sunrise occasionally.

Bet your life on Jesus. Ultimately that's the big one!

_____

Make people smile every day.

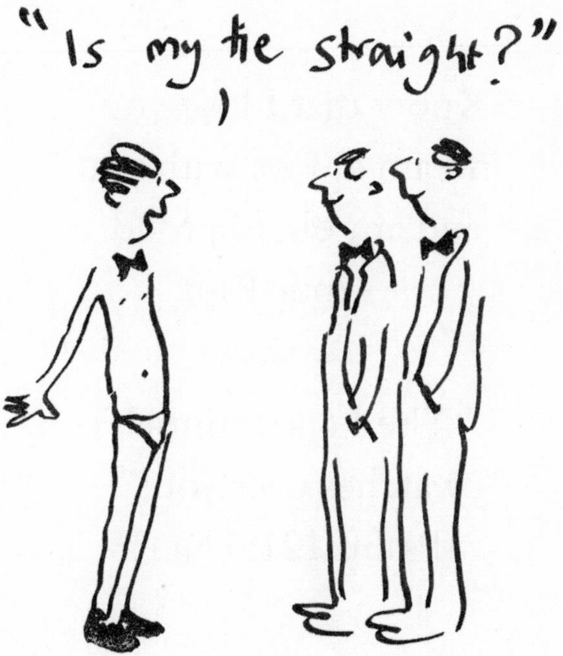
"Is my tie straight?"

Know that I love you
and am always with you
and am oh, so proud.
—Your Papa

———

"The LORD himself
watches over you!"
(Psalm 121:5 NLT)